My Wish for You

NEWMAN SPRINGS PUBLISHING
320 Broad Street
Red Bank, NJ 07701

First originally published by Newman Springs Publishing 2020

ISBN 978-1-64801-442-0 (Hardcover)
ISBN 978-1-64801-443-7 (Digital)

Printed in the United States of America

My Wish for You

j chatmon

Good morning, my love.

How did you sleep?

What wonderful things did you see in your dreams?

Were there mountains,
Or rivers,
Or valleys so green?

Were there clouds
Over oceans
That looked like ice cream?
Did the sun shine the brightest
Than it ever has shown?

Did you smile when you felt the warm wind blow?

Were there rainbows that stretched
To the end of the sky?

Or fields filled with flowers
In front of your eyes?

Did moonlight fill the night
As though it were day?
And give life to the stars
Like a thousand bouquets?

"How did you know?"

"Were you in my dreams, too?"

21

"Oh, Mama, I hope that my dreams do come true."

My dear, that is my greatest wish for you.

with the value of caregiver-child bonds and the impact these bonds can have on the growth and development of children. It is through the sharing of her own mother-son relationship in her books that j chatmon hopes others may find a similar joy as they get to know themselves through knowing their child(ren).

About the Author

j chatmon is a mother, writer, educator, vocalist, yoga-enthusiast, and more on any given day, and all before noon. Her multihyphenated interests have provided a journey through which she has created a life that feeds all of her creative energies. Writing children's books began when her son, now eight, was born, and each poem or story is an extension of the words and actions they use to enjoy this thing called life. As an educator for nearly twenty years, j chatmon is intimately familiar